GRIEG
SELECTED LYRIC PIECES

Edited and Recorded by William Westney

To access companion recorded performances online, visit:
www.halleonard.com/mylibrary

Enter Code
7627-9851-3790-0820

On the cover:
Two Ladies Walking in the Norwegian Countryside (1883)
by Fritz Thaulow
(1847–1906)

Private Collection / Photo © The Fine Art Society, London, UK / The Bridgeman Art Library

ISBN 978-1-4584-1498-4

G. SCHIRMER, Inc.

DISTRIBUTED BY
HAL•LEONARD®
CORPORATION
7777 W. BLUEMOUND RD. P.O.BOX 13819 MILWAUKEE, WI 53213

www.musicsalesclassical.com
www.halleonard.com

CONTENTS

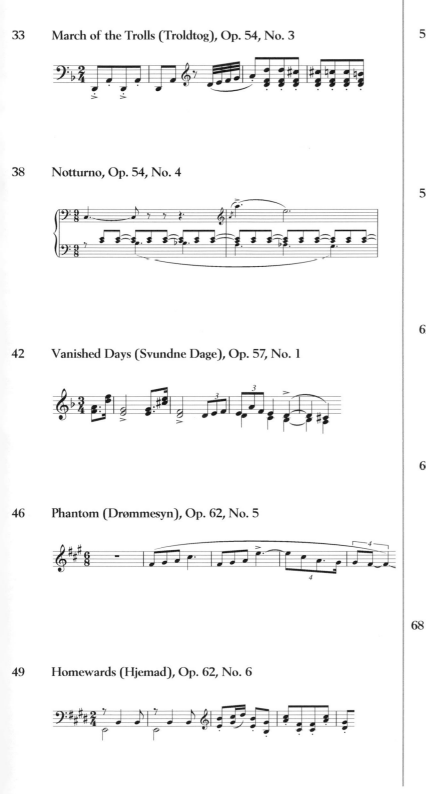

EDVARD GRIEG: LYRIC PIECES

Historical Dates of Original Publication

Opus 12	1867
Opus 38	1884
Opus 43	1886
Opus 54	1891
Opus 57	1893
Opus 62	1895
Opus 65	1897
Opus 68	1898
Opus 71	1901

SELECTED LYRIC PIECES

Relative Difficulty Levels

Intermediate
Arietta, Op. 12, No. 1
Dance of the Elves, Op. 12, No. 4
Puck, Op. 71, No. 3
Waltz, Op. 12, No. 2

Late Intermediate I
Little Bird, Op. 43, No. 4
Remembrances, Op. 71, No. 7
Shepherd Boy, Op. 54, No. 1
Solitary Traveler, Op. 43, No. 2

Late Intermediate II
Notturno, Op. 54, No. 4
To the Spring, Op. 43, No. 6
Waltz, Op. 38, No. 7

Early Advanced I
At Your Feet, Op. 68, No. 3
Butterfly, Op. 43, No. 1
March of the Trolls, Op. 54, No. 3
Phantom, Op. 62, No. 5

Early Advanced II
Homewards, Op. 62, No. 6
Vanished Days, Op. 57, No. 1
Wedding Day at Troldhaugen, Op. 65, No. 6

HISTORICAL NOTES

Edvard Grieg (1843–1907)

Though regarded as one of the great nationalist composers of the nineteenth century, Edvard Grieg had very little exposure to traditional Norwegian music as a child. He was the son of Alexander Grieg, the British consul in Bergen, Norway, a merchant and amateur orchestral musician. Edvard's mother, Gesine Hagerup, was a noted pianist and teacher of some local celebrity. The middle-class family was brought up on Beethoven, Mozart, Schumann, Weber, and Chopin under Gesine's guidance.

At the age of 15, Edvard entered the Leipzig Conservatory at the insistence of his uncle, Norwegian composer and violinist Ole Bull, who recognized the boy's unique talent at the piano. Grieg studied with Louis Plaidy, Moritz Hauptmann, Carl Reinecke, and others. The young Grieg was able to hear some of the great musicians of the time play from the newly emerging repertoire, including the recently widowed Clara Schumann, many Leipzig Gewandhaus concerts, and Wagner operas.

After graduation from the conservatory slightly delayed because of a serious bout with pleurisy, Grieg moved back to Bergen at the age of 19. Already having published two of his student works, he began to make a name for himself in his homeland as a pianist and composer of the German tradition. While on a visit to Copenhagen, Grieg came into contact with the young composer Rikard Nordraak, best remembered as the composer of the Norwegian national anthem. Nordvaak and Ole Bull introduced Grieg to the great wealth of traditional Norwegian folk melodies which would later be the source for the composer's romantic nationalist style. Unfortunately, Nordraak died suddenly of consumption at a very young age.

In 1866, Grieg gave a concert with his first cousin and future wife Nina Hagerup in Christiana (now Oslo), performing pieces by Norwegian composers, including himself and his recently deceased friend Nordraak. The concert resulted in national recognition of his talents and he was made conductor of the Philharmonic Society. The next year, he co-founded the Norwegian Academy of Music. During this time, composition of the first set of lyric pieces was completed.

Recognition came quickly. Liszt invited the Griegs to visit. Ibsen wanted to collaborate on a new play. Greig's newly-composed piano concerto was being performed internationally. Fame, along with the death of a two-year-old daughter strained the Griegs' marriage. The couple separated for six months giving Grieg the chance to travel throughout Europe, hear new works, visit other musicians, and find renewed creative focus. This hiatus and rest was exactly what the marriage as well as the creative energy of the composer needed.

In 1885, the family moved back to Bergen into a house designed by Grieg's cousin, the architect Schak Bull. The house came to be known as Troldhaugen, meaning Troll Hill, named after a nearby distinctive geographical feature, colloquially called "Troll Valley." The last twenty years of Grieg's life were spent composing, giving performances throughout Europe, and interacting with great musicians of the day including, Tchaikovsky, Brahms, Clara Schumann, Percy Grainger, Niels Gade, and many more.

Greig was an excellent pianist, and composed for the piano with a full knowledge of the instrument. Besides solo and concerto performances, he often accompanied singers (usually his wife) in his many art songs.

– Joshua Parman

PERFORMANCE NOTES

Grieg the Romantic

Piano music in Europe reached its zenith during the Romantic era of the middle to late nineteenth century. The great piano composers of that golden age all wrote music that is strikingly individual in style and uniquely recognizable. Most pianists would probably agree that this is the case not only in terms of sound but also in a physical sense—how it feels to play these works at the keyboard. Brahms' music is craggily Brahmsian, Chopin's is elegantly Chopinesque; Schumann crafted a mercurial, introspective world all his own, Rachmaninoff a luxuriant and athletic one, and so on. Where, then, does Edvard Grieg fit into such a personality-rich musical landscape?

Grieg's achievement is to have forged his own unmistakable voice while remaining true to a musical personality that was unpretentiously natural. Brahms, Chopin, Schumann and other masters of the Romantic era explored a newly expanded range of expressive possibility, and a good number of their works bespeak an intense world of unresolved yearnings, torments, desperate outcries, ambiguities, dream states, and other darkly dramatic complexities. By contrast, Grieg seems to have been a modest, sincere, gentle person who lived, on the whole, a rather contented life. There is a corresponding quality of wholesomeness and optimism in his music that makes it distinctive within the Romantic era and especially dear to music lovers; no composer has ever crafted more entertaining, imaginative and masterful character pieces than some of Grieg's greatest, such as "Butterfly," "Notturno," "To the Spring," "Wedding Day at Troldhaugen" and "March of the Trolls."

It certainly helps that Grieg had the ability to create wonderful, singable tunes that sound familiar and inevitable on first hearing—just think of *Peer Gynt*, or his great piano concerto. In general, though, the refreshing approachability of his style has never been easy to define; writers have variously described it as intimate, fragile, captivating, lyric, surprising, frisky, folkish, whimsical, and vigorous. Admittedly, Grieg's music does seem to operate within certain boundaries—some might say

limitations. Writing in the composer's own time (in 1902), American critic Daniel Gregory Mason described Grieg's art as, at heart, more "individual" than "universal." Others have pointed out that Grieg often preferred rather simple compositional procedures, such as using short phrases in somewhat predictable groupings.

Grieg's musical straightforwardness can be seen through another lens, however. National styles flourished in the Romantic era, and Grieg became—and remains—not only Norway's greatest composer but classical music's most Norwegian composer. During his creative years Norway was moving towards new political independence and solidifying its cultural identity, and Grieg's folk-flavored and accessible art reflected, and strengthened, this developing sense of what it meant to be Norwegian. His Nordic aesthetic, and his devotion to tonality and warm-hearted lyricism, held fast even towards the end of the century, when other composers such as Scriabin, Liszt and Strauss were beginning to experiment with post-tonal and post-Romantic musical realms.

The Lyric Pieces

For many piano composers, short character pieces are expressions of a rather personal nature when compared with more formal works like sonatas. In Grieg's case, what these musical miniatures reveal is his immediacy of expression and his love of Nordic nature and folklore. The Lyric Pieces make perfect assignments for a blossoming young pianist who is just beginning to discover his or her technical ability, interpretive voice, and the gratification that comes from performing selections that are short, accessible, and that can captivate an audience. Adult amateur pianists will also find them satisfying, since many of these works express feelings of a certain maturity and seem to have been written for fairly large hands. While several of the pieces are challenging technically and make a brilliant effect, they are generally not unduly difficult and are always comfortably pianistic.

The pieces for this edition have been selected for their quality and variety, ranging from the first opus to the last, and encompassing a mixture of genres, moods and levels of difficulty. It should be noted that Grieg's musical style does evolve interestingly over time; in some of the later works, for example "At Your Feet" (Op. 68, No. 3), he is clearly experimenting, deftly and expressively, with harmonic ambiguity, chromaticism and sudden modulation. Throughout the series, whatever the style or mood of the piece in question, his vivid titles conjure a colorful world that inspires the imagination of performer and audience alike.

Both the very first Lyric Piece ("Arietta") and the last ("Remembrances") have been included in this volume, and for a special reason: Grieg decided opus 71 would be his last set of Lyric Pieces, and took the charming and unusual step of rounding off the entire series by coming back quite literally to where it all started. "Remembrances" quotes the melody of the first piece, thirty-four years later, but now extends it with a different meter, dreamlike changes of key, and a floating last measure that doesn't sound final at all, but rather suggests that the lyric impulse flows on eternally.

About This Edition

Wherever possible, Grieg's original expressive indications—pedaling, phrasing, articulation, dynamics, metronome markings—have been preserved, with editorial suggestions shown in brackets. Fingering is that of the current editor.

A note on legato: For many years piano pedagogues insisted that one must execute note-to-note finger legato whenever possible. This has often led editors to suggest fingerings that are in fact quite weak and awkward, that stretch the hand into distorted positions, or that introduce needless complexities such as fussy finger substitutions on a single piano key all in the service of literally connecting one note to the next using only the fingers. In the current edition, however, many of the melodic phrases have deliberately been given non-legato fingerings, even when the composer writes a slur marking. The theory here is that in a richly harmonic style such as Grieg's in which generous amounts of pedal are in use it is simply not always necessary to connect one finger to another. More importantly, what makes legato lyricism truly "sing" is a pianistic voice of fullness and warmth, and this can best be produced when the hand is in a comfortable position and the

arm is actively involved. This means that shorter phrases are sometimes better than long ones since they allow the arm to lift more frequently, drop into the keys again using strong fingers, and thus renew and maintain depth of singing tone. Since control of sound is much easier to achieve when the body is comfortable, a pianist can readily create the effect of a long, beautifully-shaped melodic line even while playing it (technically) as several shorter segments.

Another area in which the editor advises a not-too-literal approach is that of dynamics. One of the trickiest skills for developing pianists to master is that of playing softly without losing quality and projection of tone. When students respond to indications of *piano* and *pianissimo* by retreating and playing timidly and on the surface (lest they be told they are "too loud") the result will be a colorless, unreliable tone that does not communicate well to a listener. Far better to treat all dynamics on a grand scale and to realize that quiet passages need to be just as tonally healthy and beautiful as the louder ones in order to project with eloquence. In this view, dynamics are more suggestive of mood and color than they are of strict contrasts between loud and soft. Additionally, one often sees in these pieces, as in most music of the era, long undifferentiated stretches indicated with a single dynamic such as *pianissimo* or *forte*. This can best be understood as a kind of notational shorthand on the part of composers, and doesn't actually mean that the level of sound should be uniform throughout. Romantic music will be more alive and pleasing when dynamics are in a state of movement; for example, when the performer thinks of a series of small crescendos through the phrases, as is suggested in this edition from time to time.

Notes on the Individual Pieces

Arietta, Op. 12, No. 1 (composed 1867)

The elegant, simple and natural melody of "Arietta" introduces the set of miniatures that comprise the Lyric Pieces. Its musical material will return in the same key but in altered form in the last piece as well. Although the dynamic is marked *piano* throughout, feel free to sing out the top line with warm soloistic richness.

Waltz (Vals), Op. 12, No. 2 (composed 1866)

This Waltz, with its moderate tempo and haunting Nordic quality, springs to life when the articulations in the melody—staccatos, tenutos, accents—are made vigorously and crisply clear. Crossing the right and left hands in the major section, as suggested, is quite a comfortable and logical choice pianistically.

Dance of the Elves (Elverdans), Op. 12, No. 4 (composed 1867)

"Elves' Dance" is one of the numerous Lyric Pieces that conjure up the fantastical world of Nordic supernatural creatures. While much of the piece is marked *pianissimo*, it is actually more effective when played with more varied and textured dynamics, such as those suggested by the editor.

Waltz (Vals), Op. 38, No. 7 (composed 1866, rev. 1883)

The opening phrase, although slurred over four measures, can in fact be played more lyrically, i.e. with better tone and shape, when one divides it into two phrases as suggested. Doing so simply permits the pianist to find much more comfortable hand positions, and makes stronger fingers available for the melody.

Butterfly (Sommerfugl), Op. 43, No. 1 (composed 1886)

Nature-inspired and highly sophisticated in every way, this is one of Grieg's most cherished masterpieces. Play it flexibly, spontaneously, and not too fast; the stylish and pianistic writing will do most of the work for you. A dynamic marking like the *sff* in measure 39 seems a bit over-notated by the composer; we should certainly take note of the spirit behind it, but not feel obligated to play it quite so violently.

Solitary Traveler (Ensom Vandrer), Op. 43, No. 2 (composed 1886)

Unadorned and melancholic, this eloquent piece shines when performed with full melodic tone and a flexible, *parlando* approach to tempo. In double-note passages like that in measure 3, it is sufficient to connect only one of the notes, usually the top.

Little Bird (Liden Fugl), Op. 43, No. 4 (composed 1886)

Another masterwork, this delightful and virtuosic bonbon shows Grieg's comprehensive understanding of pianistic idiom and technique. Achieving perfect rhythmic precision between the hands in the 32nd-note flourishes creates such a scintillating effect that there is no need to play the piece at a very fast tempo. Unhurried clarity is the key to brilliance here.

To the Spring (Til Foråret), Op. 43, No. 6 (composed 1886)

In addition to its remarkable and rapturous atmosphere, "To the Spring" offers one of Romanticism's most memorable and well-known melodies. When the tune is doubled beginning in measure 23, bringing out the left hand more prominently than the right can color the expression a bit more darkly and heighten the air of mysterious anticipation.

Shepherd Boy (Gjærtergut), Op. 54, No. 1 (composed 1891)

Despite its pastoral title and subject, this piece is moody and quite adventurous harmonically, with modulations that sound almost Wagnerian in the middle section. Also unusual and of note in the middle part is the quasi-improvisational rhythmic character in the right hand.

March of the Trolls (Troldtog), Op. 54, No. 3 (composed 1891)

Colorful Nordic folklore and bravura pianism are artfully combined here to forge a spooky and brilliant showpiece. As tempting as it might be to tear into the (not very difficult) first page as fast as possible, Grieg was quite right to call for a true *allegro moderato*. As with many of his pieces, choosing a not-too-quick speed helps bring out the music's intriguing atmosphere and humor. Even more practically, doing so in this piece makes it possible for the leaping *fortissimo* octaves at measure 40 to explode thrillingly and accurately with no flagging of tempo. The rapid four-note figures that permeate the melody can also be executed, when the pace is unhurried, with a crystalline clarity that lends the piece real shivers of excitement. The editor recommends no change of tempo for the middle part, starting in measure 71. Keep the lyric phrases moving and don't sentimentalize them.

Notturno, Op. 54, No. 4 (composed 1891)

This favorite of the concert stage is one of the most inspired and justifiably famous of the Lyric Pieces. Notable for its beautiful harmonic changes, the intimate Romantic texture of its gently pulsating chords and the sincerity of its very singable melody, this is music that generally transcends the boundaries of national styles. The only remnant of Nordic flavor we find is the downward melodic leap of a third, as in measure 4, a small detail that is a signature element of Grieg's style. Also clearly Griegian is the charming nature depictions in the middle section, evoking lilting birdsong and evening sounds that echo from one mountaintop to another.

Vanished Days (Svundne Dage), Op. 57, No. 1 (composed 1893)

In many of the later Lyric Pieces, Grieg heightens the emotional intensity through strong use of chromaticism. That is certainly the case in this rustic story of nostalgia for the innocence and gaiety (almost desperate at times) of days gone by.

Phantom (Drømmesyn), Op. 62, No. 5 (composed 1895)

Stylistic creativity characterizes "Phantom." Nordic traits are absent, harmonies are shifting chromatically, phrases are longer than usual, chords are rarely encountered in root position, and a dreamily sophisticated mood prevails. Play this piece imaginatively and freely.

Homewards (Hjemad), Op. 62, No. 6 (composed 1895)

This merry and spirited vignette of country life is by no means an easy piece technically. Grieg's suggestion of a measured *alla marcia* tempo is just right; one might even consider counting it in 4 instead of in 2 to achieve clarity in the right-hand figures and accuracy in the left-hand jumps starting in measure 27.

Wedding Day at Troldhaugen (Bryllupsdag på Troldhaugen), Op. 65, No. 6 (composed 1897)

There can hardly be a more surefire and exhilarating character piece in all of piano music than "Wedding Day at Troldhaugen," with its inspired melodies, sly wit, exciting buildup of dynamics, sunny atmosphere, and its extroverted brilliance. Even better, it is a fine example of the sort of work pianists most love to perform: something that manages to sound just a bit more difficult to play than it really is.

Here again, Grieg steers us in the right direction tempo-wise, recommending a march-feeling in 4 that should only be "a bit" lively. All too often one hears this piece start off far too quickly, which leads to messy and frantic passages later on and robs the music of its good-humored charm. The editor advises only a slight relaxation of tempo for the middle section, which seems to depict a tender and intimate conversation. Much of the change of mood is already written into this contrasting part, thanks to its droning pedal point and the calmer note values in all voices. Thus it's best not to slow down very much, since doing so might detract from the festive joy that permeates the entire composition.

At Your Feet (For dine Føtter), Op. 68, No. 3 (composed 1898)

Expansive lines, passionate expression and skillful chromaticism characterize this little-known and subtle gem. It is universal in style—Norwegian touches are nowhere to be found.

Puck (Småtrold), Op. 71, No. 3 (composed 1901)

This is vintage Grieg, with its dark, impish fairy-tale character and the sly humor created by its suspenseful mood and the sudden changes in dynamics. Play it with dramatic zest and communicate your enjoyment to your listeners.

Remembrances (Efterklang), Op. 71, No. 7 (composed 1901)

We now return to (literally "remember") the very first lyric piece. It has been transformed into a gentle waltz of fond nostalgia, in which harmonies drift from one key to another with dreamy whimsicality.

Instead of a full chordal accompaniment at the start, this time we hear only a single note, the soprano "G" floating alone, timelessly, with a *fermata*. The piece ends in just the same way, with the same sweet, isolated held note in the treble. Time is a circle, this seems to say, and the lyric impulse goes on forever.

– *William Westney*

Notes

[1] Daniel Gregory Mason, *From Grieg to Brahms* (New York: Macmillan, 1902), 67.

SELECTED LYRIC PIECES

Arietta

Edvard Grieg
Op. 12, No. 1

Poco andante e sostenuto [♩ = 63–69]

Waltz
(Vals)

Edvard Grieg
Op. 12, No. 2

*One might consider omitting the initial C-sharp from the left-hand chord in measures 39 and 47.

Dance of the Elves
(Elverdans)

Edvard Grieg
Op. 12, No. 4

Molto allegro e sempre staccato [♩. = 92–96]

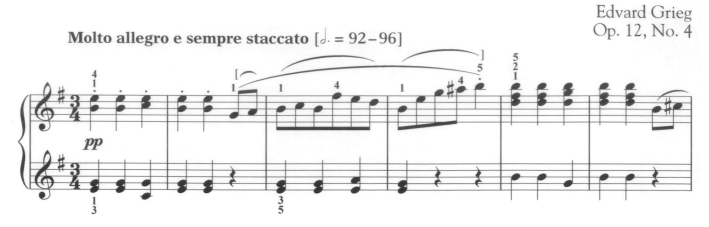

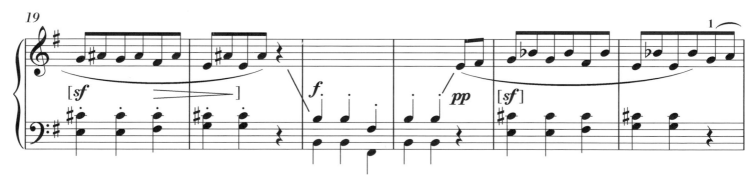

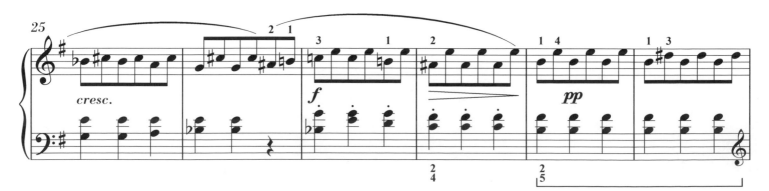

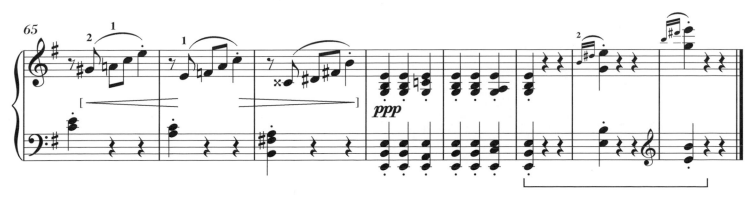

Waltz
(Vals)

Edvard Grieg
Op. 38, No. 7

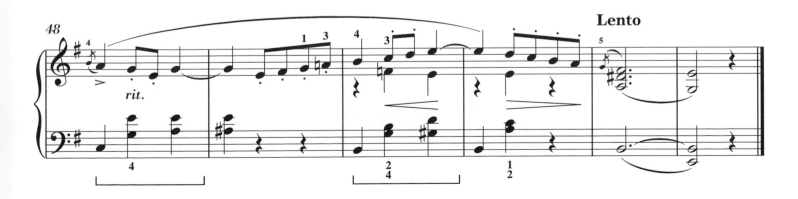

Butterfly
(Sommerfugl)

Edvard Grieg
Op. 43, No. 1

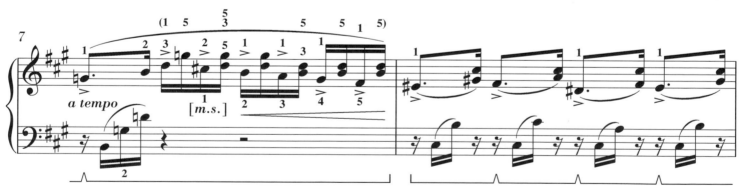

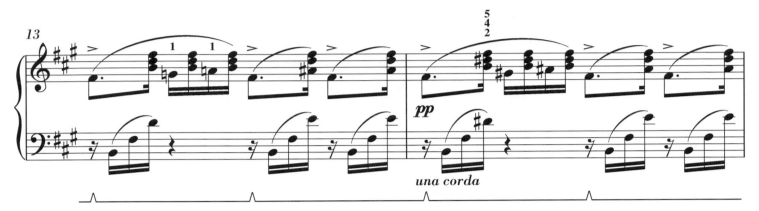

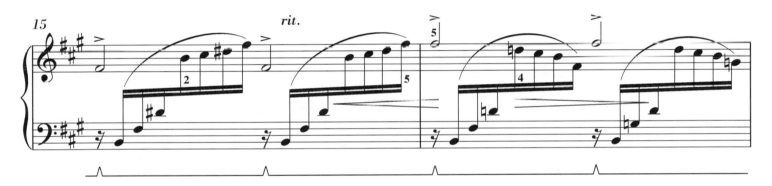

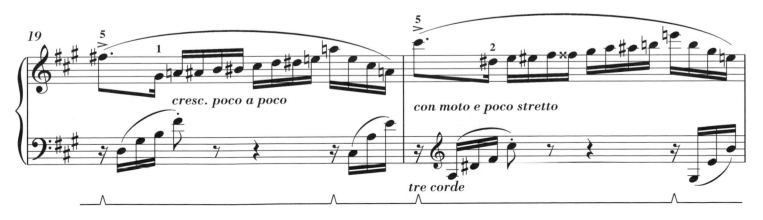

20

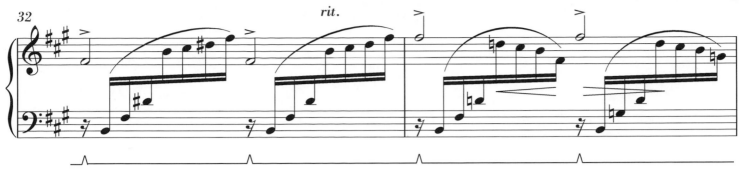

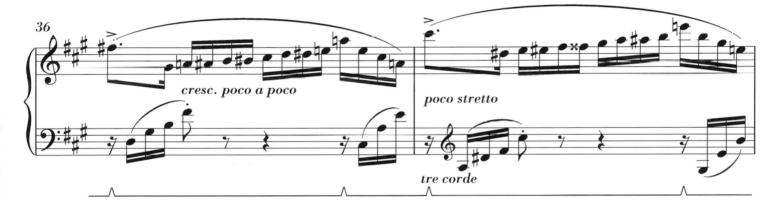

Solitary Traveler
(Ensom Vandrer)

Edvard Grieg
Op. 43, No. 2

Allegretto semplice ♪ = 116 [♪ = 138]

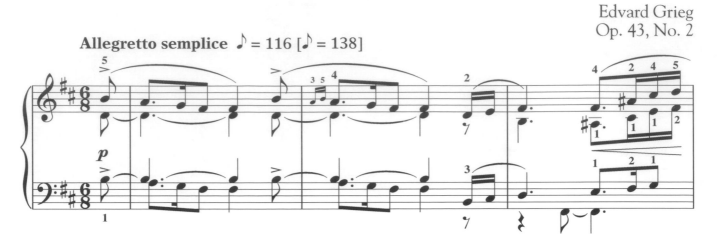

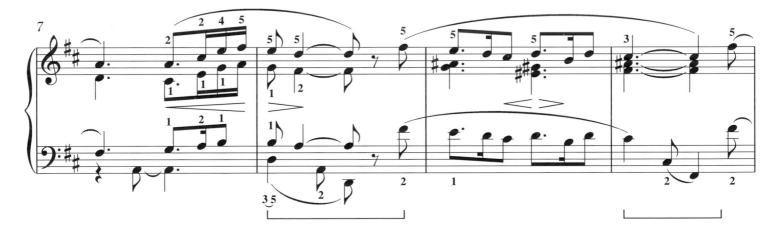

Little Bird
(Liden Fugl)

Edvard Grieg
Op. 43, No. 4

Allegro leggiero ♩. = 88 [♩. = 80 – 88]

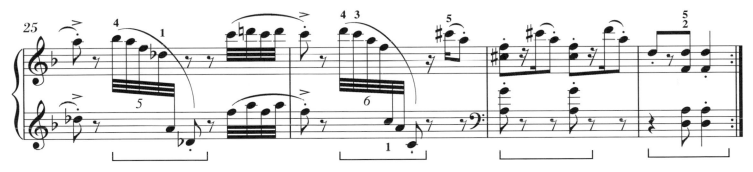

To the Spring
(Til Foråret)

Edvard Grieg
Op. 43, No. 6

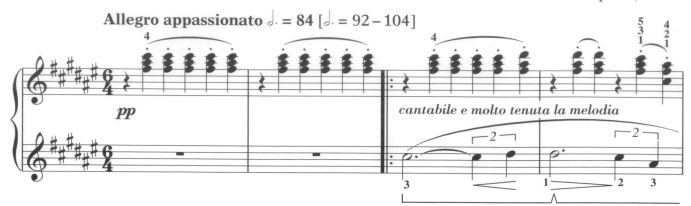

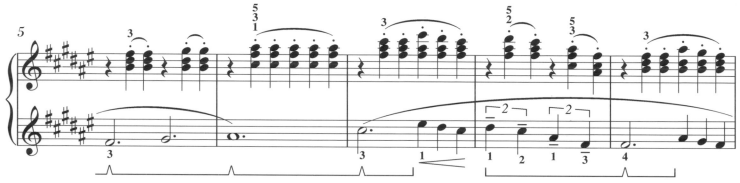

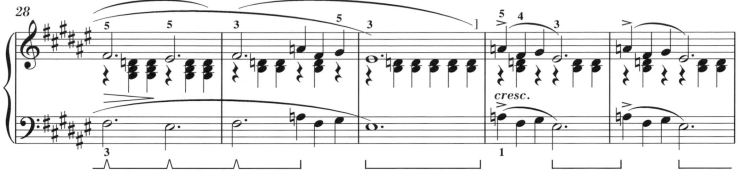

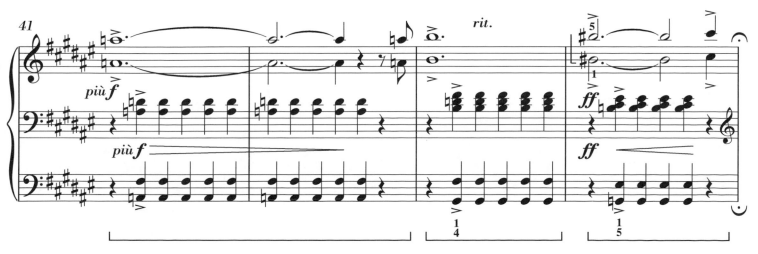

Tempo I [A tempo, ma poco meno mosso]

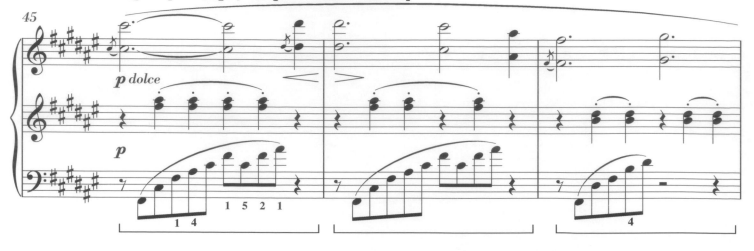

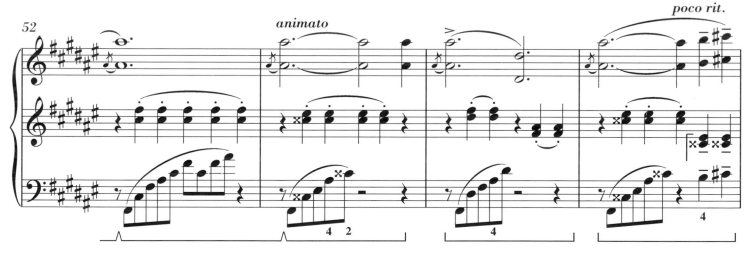

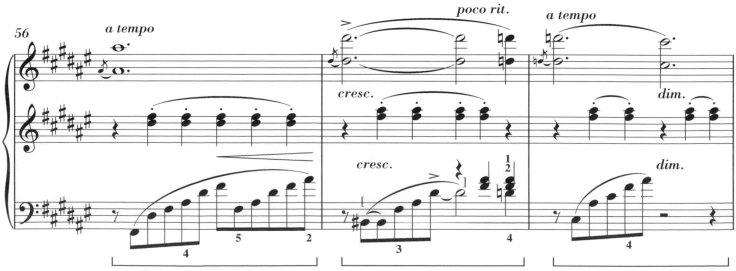

Shepherd Boy
(Gjærtergut)

Edvard Grieg
Op. 54, No. 1

Andante espressivo [♩. = 60 – 66]

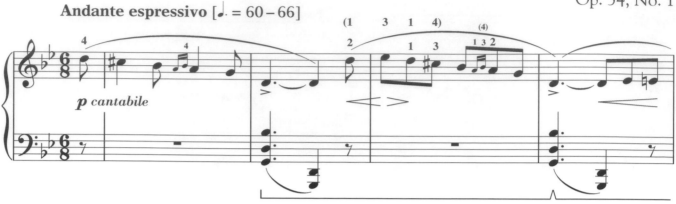

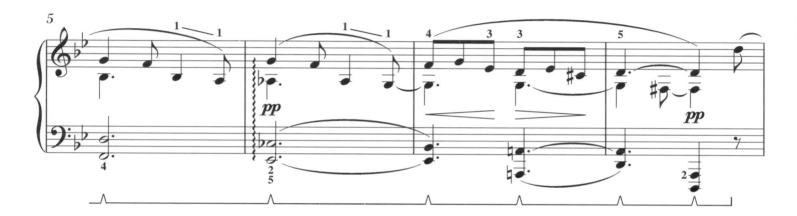

Poco mosso

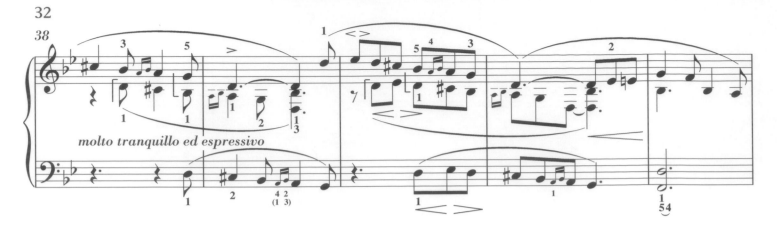

molto tranquillo ed espressivo

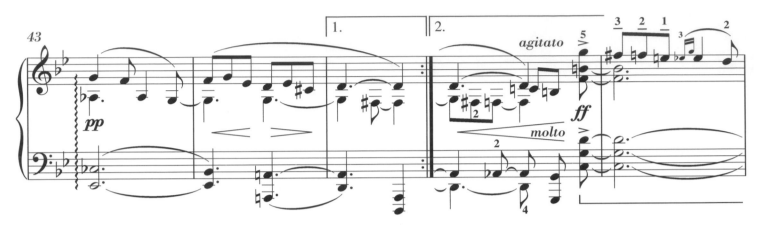

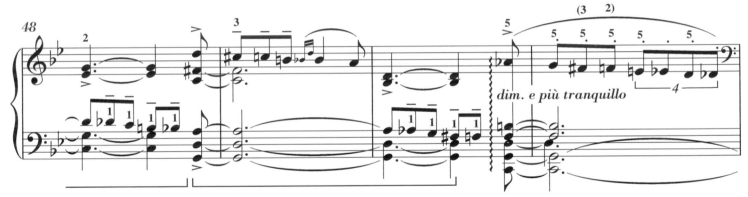

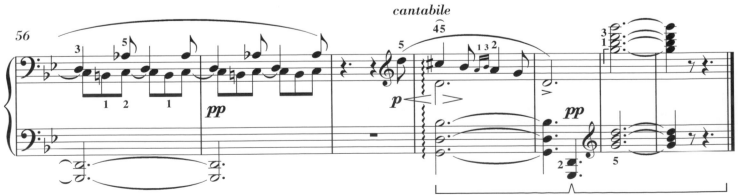

March of the Trolls
(Troldtog)

Edvard Grieg
Op. 54, No. 3

Allegro moderato [♩ = 126–132]

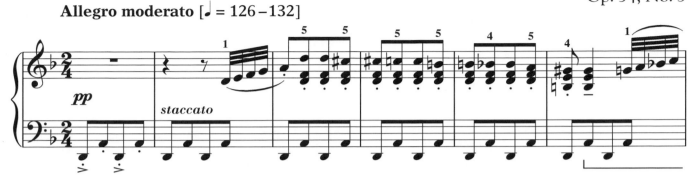

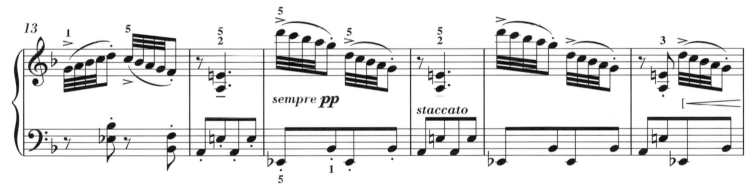

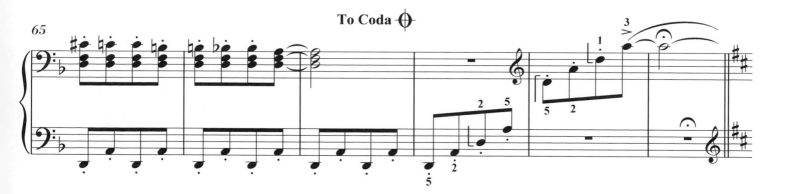

[l'istesso tempo]

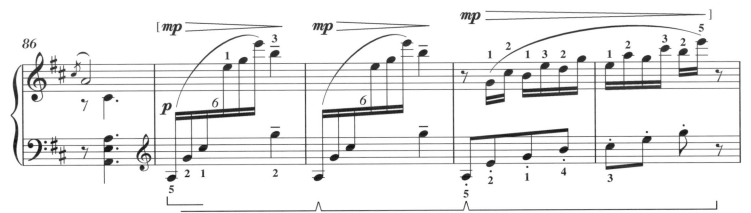

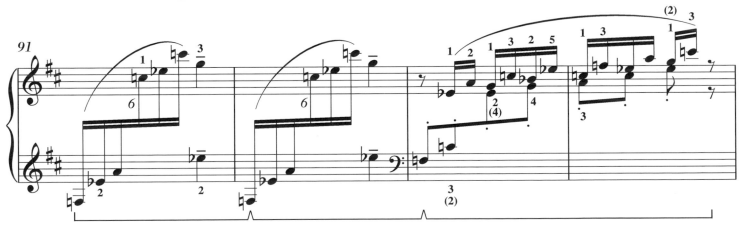

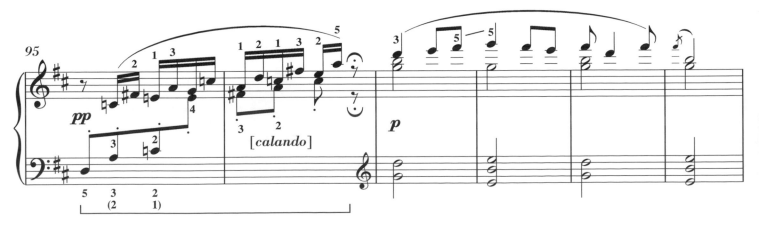

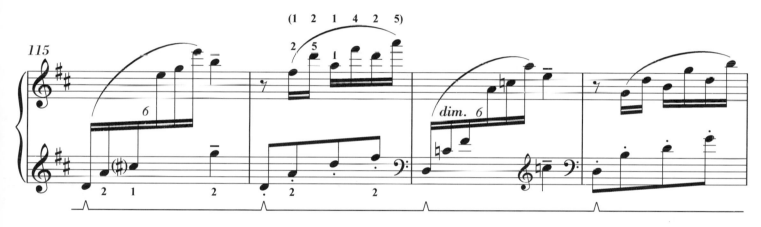

D.C. al Coda

CODA

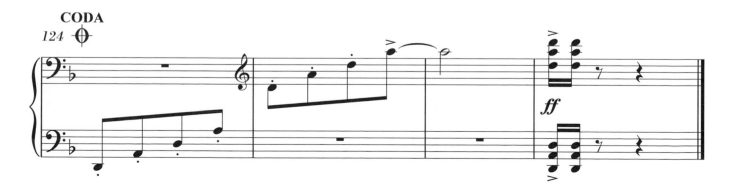

Notturno

Edvard Grieg
Op. 54, No. 4

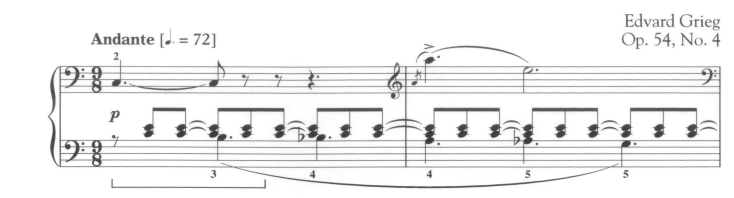

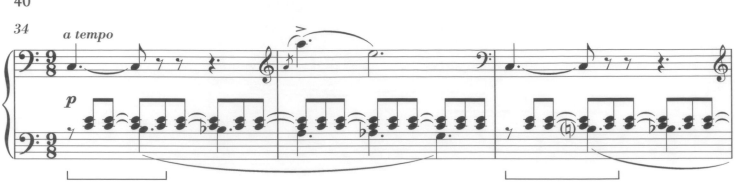

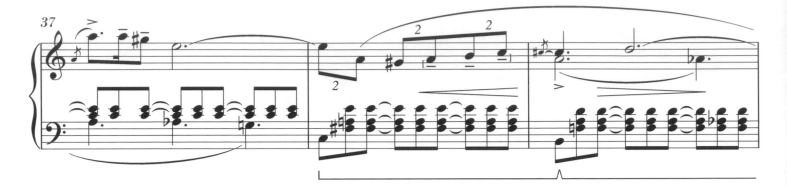

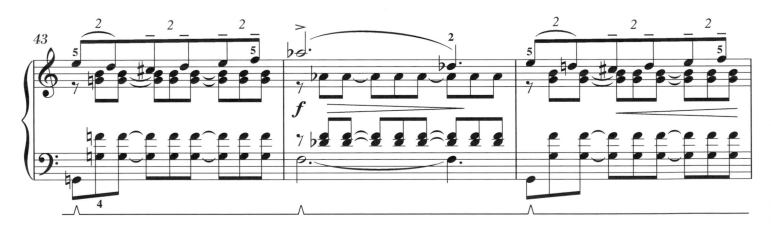

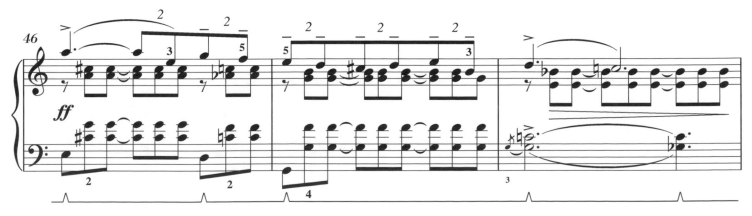

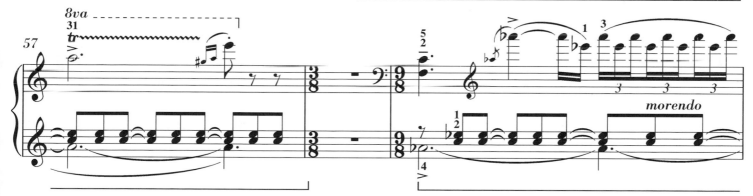

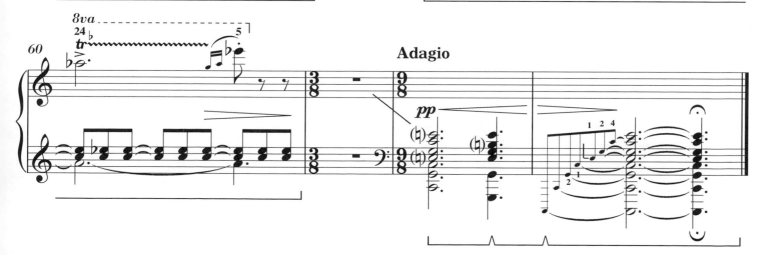

Vanished Days
(Svundne Dage)

Edvard Grieg
Op. 57, No. 1

Andantino [very freely] [♩ = 72–80]

44

Phantom
(Drømmesyn)

Edvard Grieg
Op. 62, No. 5

Poco andante ed espressivo [♩. = 76]

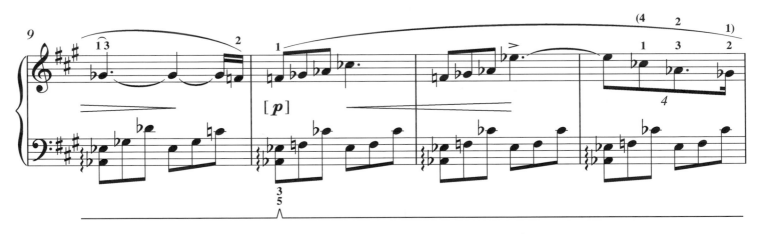

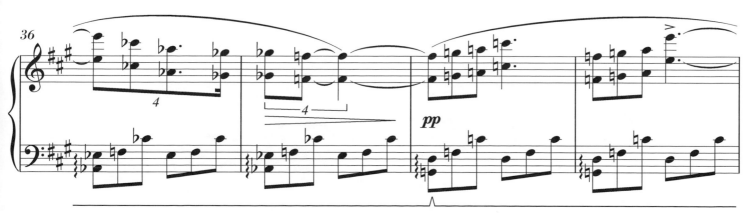

48

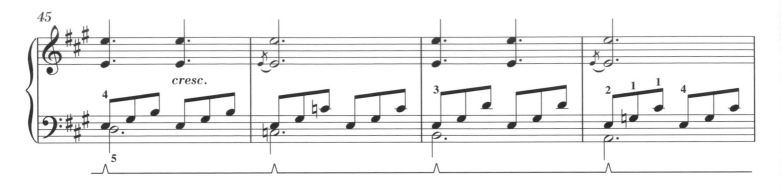

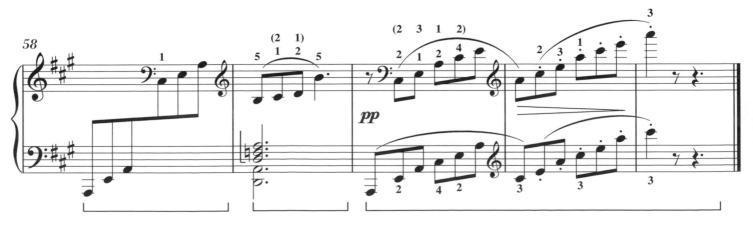

Homewards
(Hjemad)

Edvard Grieg
Op. 62, No. 6

Allegro giocoso alla marcia [♩ = 104–108]

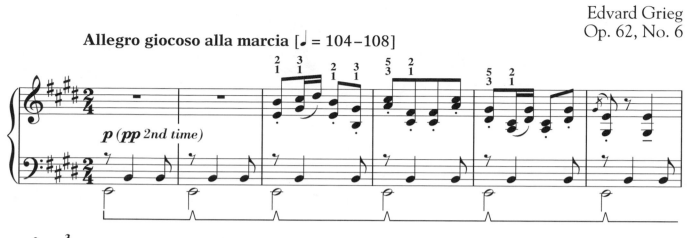

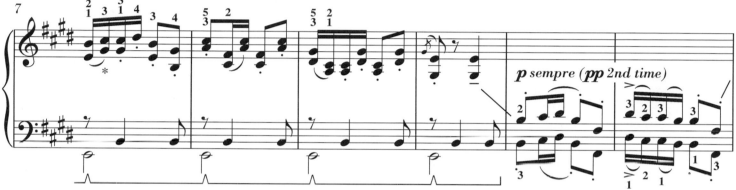

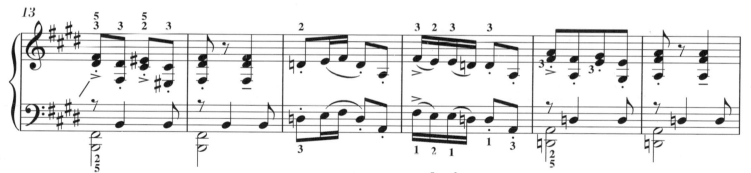

*For clarity and easier execution, the G-sharp may be omitted.

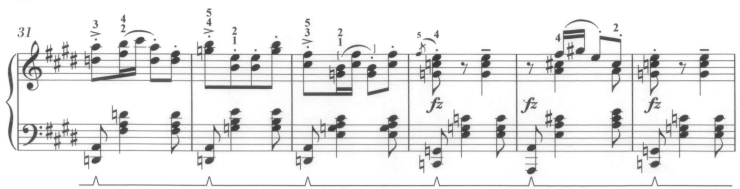

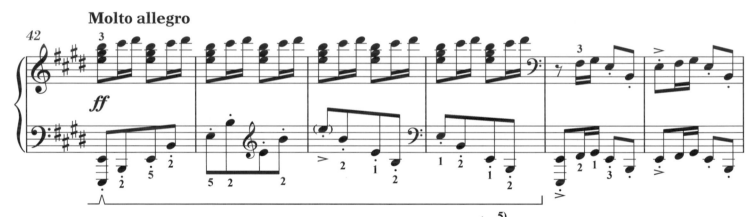

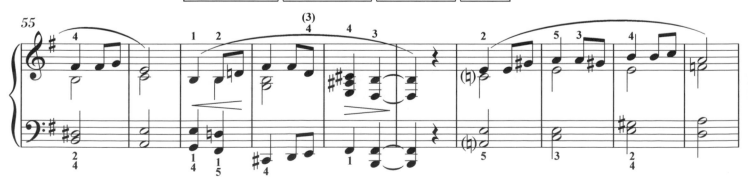

CODA Molto allegro

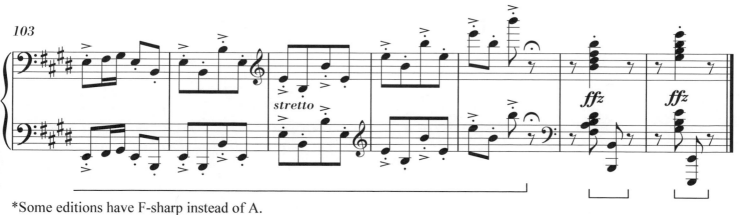

*Some editions have F-sharp instead of A.

Wedding Day at Troldhaugen
(Bryllupsdag på Troldhaugen)

Edvard Grieg
Op. 65, No. 6

Tempo di Marcia un poco vivace [♩ = 112 –120]

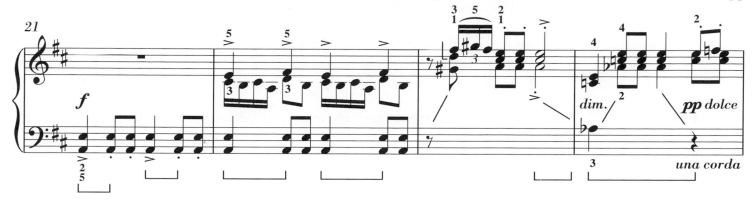

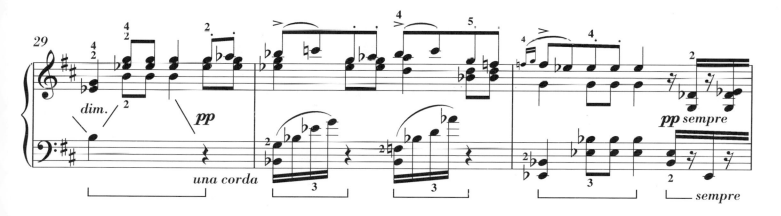

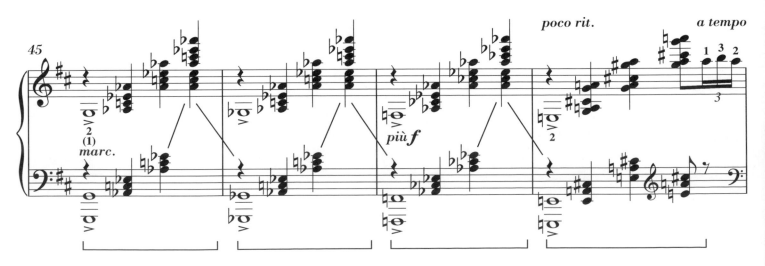

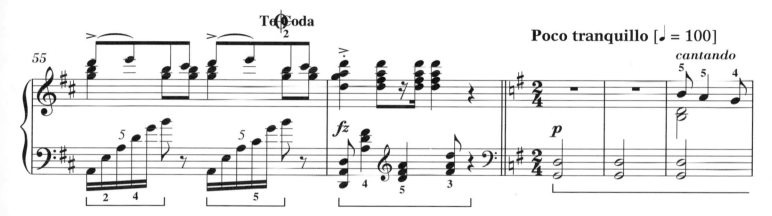

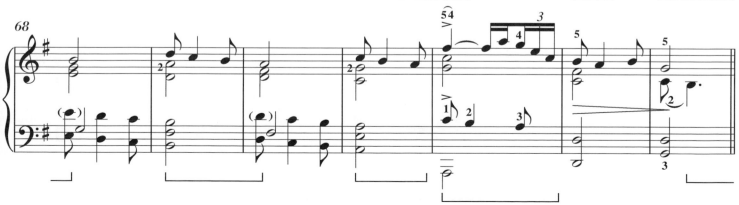

CODA

At Your Feet

(For dine Føtter)

Edvard Grieg
Op. 68, No. 3

Poco andante e molto espressivo [♩ = 104 – 112]

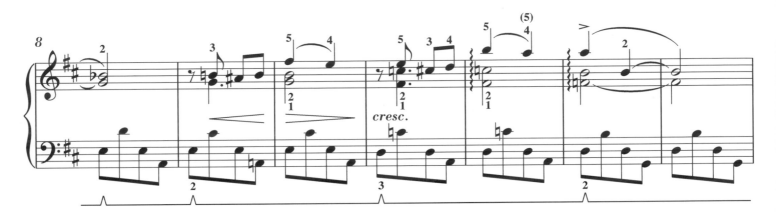

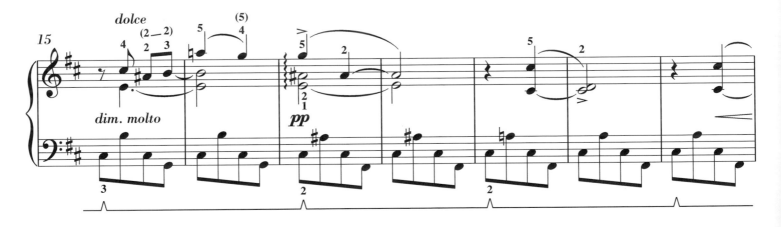

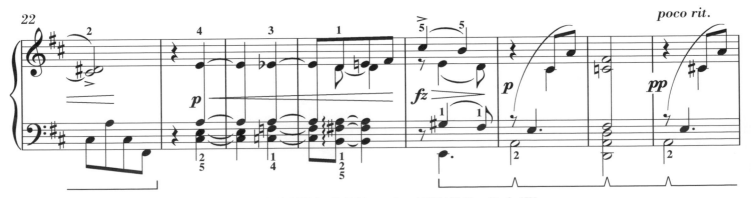

60

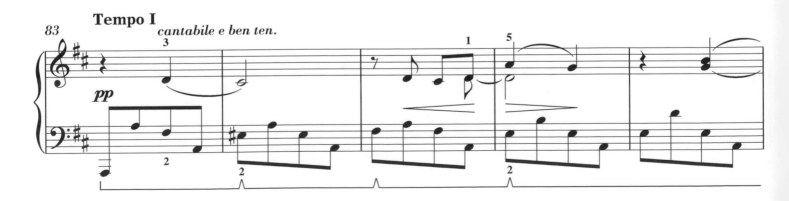

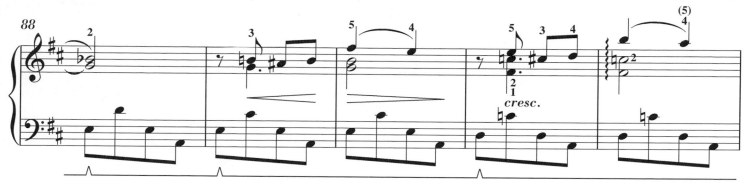

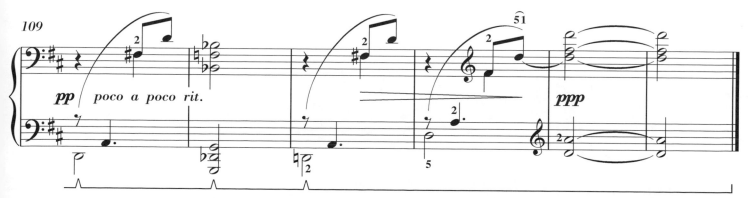

Puck
(Småtrold)

Edvard Grieg
Op. 71, No. 3

*Some editions have C-natural.

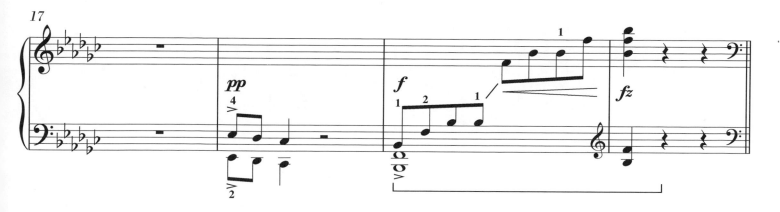

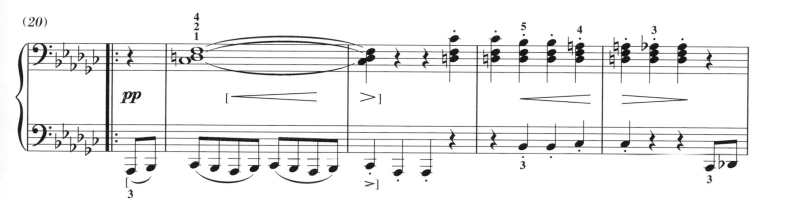

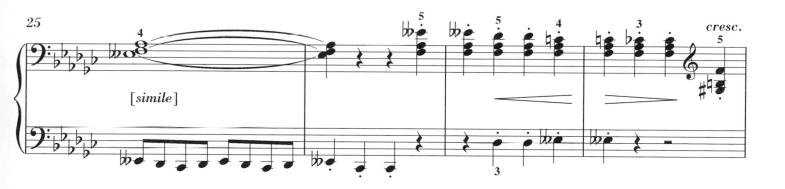

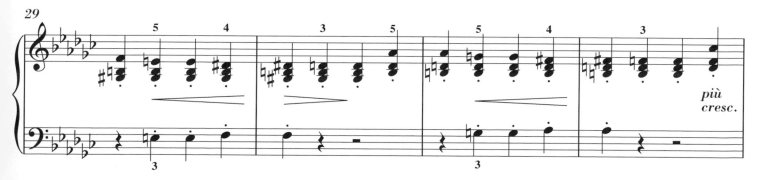

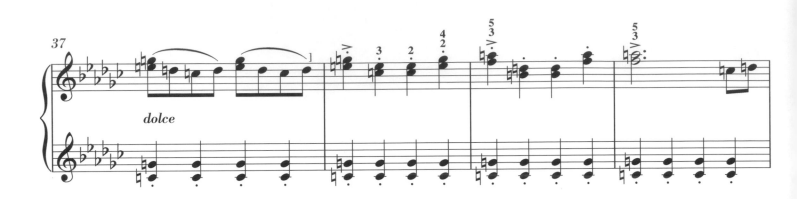

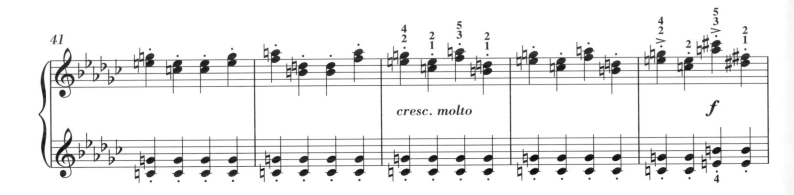

Remembrances
(Efterklang)

Edvard Grieg
Op. 71, No. 7

Tempo di Valse [♩. = 60–66]

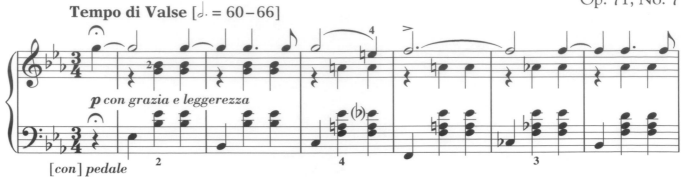

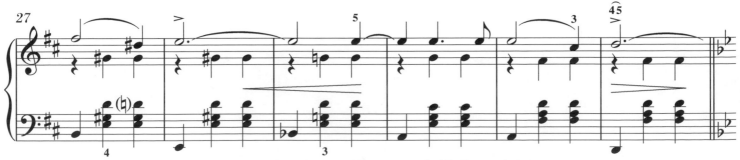

ABOUT THE EDITOR

WILLIAM WESTNEY

William Westney brings notable credentials as both performer and pedagogue to this project. He was the top piano prizewinner in the Geneva International Competition and holds a Doctor of Musical Arts degree from Yale University School of Music. He has soloed with such major orchestras as the Houston Symphony and L'Orchestre de la Suisse Romande, toured on three continents, and his recording of music by Leo Ornstein was cited in *Newsweek* magazine's "Top 10" list. Currently a Paul Whitfield Horn Distinguished Professor and the Browning Artist-in-Residence at Texas Tech University, he has held guest professorships in Denmark and Taiwan, taught in Korea as a Fulbright Senior Scholar (U.S. State Department), and won many teaching awards including the highest Texas Tech can bestow (Chancellor's Council Distinguished Teaching Award). Among the venues for the hundreds of workshops he has given internationally are Central Conservatory (Beijing), Sibelius Academy (Helsinki), Royal College of Music (London), University of Music and the Performing Arts (Vienna), Royal Danish Academy of Music (Copenhagen), Victorian College for the Arts (Melbourne), Kennedy Center for the Performing Arts (Washington, DC), The Juilliard School (New York), and many more. Westney is noted for his unique "Un-Master Class" workshop, described as "fascinating" in a N.Y. Times feature article, and is the author of the best-selling and critically acclaimed book *The Perfect Wrong Note* (2003). He was the artist/editor for two prior volumes in the "Schirmer Performance Editions" series—etudes by Burgmüller and Heller—and served for four years as Chair of the Editorial Committee for *American Music Teacher* magazine. Westney's pedagogical work was the focus and cover story of the May/June 2009 issue of *Clavier Companion* magazine, and in 2012 he was given the Frances Clark Keyboard Pedagogy Award by Music Teachers National Association for "significant contributions" to the field.